GUITAR NOCTURNES

BY WILLIAM BAY

ISBN 978-09888327-1-8

© 2013 BY WILLIAM BAY
ALL RIGHTS RESERVED. INTERNATIONAL COPYRIGHT SECURED. B.M.I.

Visit us on the Web at www.williambaymusic.com

PREFACE

I have always loved the contemplative, introspective nature of nocturnes. The pieces in this collection are very lyrical, melodic solos, intermediate in difficulty and composed in keys which sound rich and full on the guitar. They should be played freely with a maximum of expression. Feel free to vary the tempos as needed.

The solos are andante to adagio in tempo and should be performed in a relaxed, unhurried manner. They will be appropriate in a variety of concert settings.

I have always believed that the plectrum or flatpick guitar could be an exciting concert instrument. It is with this in mind that I have written and recorded numerous items in the **William Bay Music** catalog. These items may be found on my website: ***williambaymusic.com***.

I hope you enjoy playing these pieces as much as I enjoyed composing them!

William Bay

CONTENTS

Nocturne #1 in A minor — 4

Nocturne #2 in E minor — 7

Nocturne #3 in D minor — 10

Nocturne #4 in A minor — 14

Nocturne #5 in E minor — 18

Nocturne #6 in A Major — 22

Nocturne #7 in F♯ minor — 26

Nocturne #8 in D minor — 30

Nocturne #9 in E Major — 33

Nocturne #10 in D Major — 36

Nocturne #11 in A minor — 40

Nocturne #12 in D Major — 44

NOCTURNE 1/ A MINOR

William Bay

© 2013 by William Bay. All Rights Reserved. BMI.

NOCTURNE 2/E MINOR

William Bay

NOCTURNE 3/ D MINOR

Dropped D Tuning

William Bay

This page has been left blank
to avoid awkward page turns.

NOCTURNE 4/A MINOR

NOCTURNE 5/ E MINOR

William Bay

NOCTURNE 6/A MAJOR

William Bay

This page has been left blank
to avoid awkward page turns.

NOCTURNE 7/F# MINOR

William Bay

29

NOCTURNE 8/D MINOR

NOCTURNE 9/ E MAJOR

William Bay

NOCTURNE 10/D MAJOR

Dropped D Tuning

William Bay

NOCTURNE 11/A MINOR

© 2013 by William Bay. All Rights Reserved. BMI.

This page has been left blank to avoid awkward page turns.

NOCTURNE 12/D MAJOR

© 2013 by William Bay. All Rights Reserved. BMI.

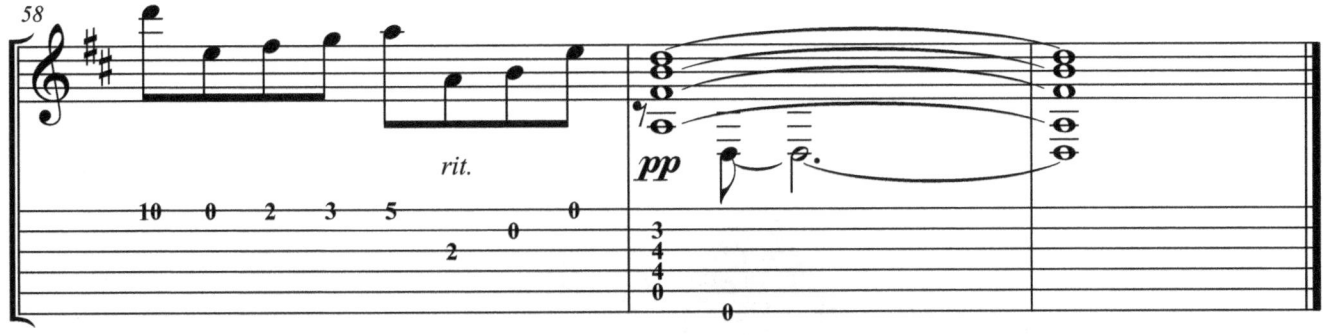

www.williambaymusic.com

www.ingramcontent.com/pod-product-compliance
Lightning Source LLC
LaVergne TN
LVHW061256060426
835507LV00020B/2336